THE EMPERORS

The
EMPERORS

FRANK MANLEY

Turtle Point Press

NEW YORK

ISBN 1-885586-19-1

LCCN 00-136360

Design and composition by
Wilsted & Taylor Publishing Services
Front cover photograph by Jerry Uelsmann

Acknowledgment is made to the editors of *Poetry* for permission to reprint "Heliogabalus," the third poem in the sequence on Antoninus Elagabalus; to the editors of the *Sewanee Review* for "Julius," "Zenobia," and the third poem in the sequence on Hadrian; to the *Cumberland Poetry Review* for "Antoninus Pius"; and to the *Chattahoochee Review* for "Claudius" and "Elagabalus," the first poem in the sequence on Antoninus Elagabalus. The Latin is taken from Suetonius and the *Scriptores Historiae Augustae*. Translations are by the author.

For we are not contending against flesh and blood,
but against the principalities, against the powers,
against the world rulers of this present darkness, against
the spiritual hosts of wickedness in the heavenly places.

EPHESIANS 6:12

CONTENTS

INTRODUCTION

There were only a couple of times in my life when I was able to write poetry. I taught it on a regular basis. I read it for pleasure, wrote critical essays about it, and even regarded myself as an expert without ever having tried to do it myself, not even as an adolescent, when almost everyone is driven to it by sex and hormonal changes and adolescent despair and the sort of feelings immortalized in popular songs. I had not tried partly from modesty, believing that I wouldn't be able to do it, and partly from fear, not wanting to make a fool of myself. I was no artist—I knew that. I was a grown man of eighteen who had nothing but contempt for the self-absorbed, hand-to-mouth existence of artists. Maturity, as I defined it then, consisted of compliance with the world and the rational acceptance of one's own limitations. I wanted to marry. I wanted to live a simple, ordinary life. And so, in my innocence, I became a university professor.

And then, almost twenty years later, when I was in my mid-thirties, I felt as though my life was coming apart. I was a reasonably respectable citizen, a dutiful husband, the father of two lovely daughters, the chairman of the department in which I taught. But I no longer knew what I was doing or why I was doing it. I had lost faith in most things except for my family and, at times, an enormous volume I was editing for the Yale edition of the *Complete Works* of St. Thomas More. And teaching—sometimes I found something of value there. But most of the time I felt like a priest who had lost his religion and was simply going through the motions.

I remember once, for example, when Hubert Humphrey was scheduled to speak on campus. This was during the war in Vietnam, and Humphrey was vice president at the time— or a presidential candidate. I can't remember which. Anyway, rumor had it that the students intended to drown Humphrey out by chanting anti-war slogans during his speech, and the dean of the college, one of my old professors and a good friend of mine, was equally intent on stopping them. The dean was a genuinely upright man, a model of old fashioned virtue and decorum, who believed that the university, more than most places, had the duty to protect free speech. The students' protest, he thought, was against all reason, against all civic and moral virtue, against all the principles our country was founded on. He did not realize that it was precisely that sort of pious humbug in the face of the deaths of so many young men and the great deception of the war itself that made the students want to protest in the first place. A country that could mouth so many moral platitudes and at the same time do so much to violate its own basic principles seemed like the greatest hypocrisy.

Around 6:00 p.m. on the day that Humphrey was scheduled to speak, I received a call from the dean telling me that he had called an emergency meeting of the chairs of all departments. We were to meet in his office immediately. As soon as we arrived, the dean described what the students intended to do and told us that it was our job to stop them. He acted as though we were a council of war, a group of generals and high-ranking officers called together to plan a campaign, and I felt like a spy or traitor, or worse. I believed in free speech. I believed in the principles on which this country was founded. But I also agreed with what the students were doing. The government was lying to us. Why should we listen to them? They were surely not listening to us. This was not a free debate. It was more complex and confusing than that. I no longer had (if I ever did) the same sort of simple-minded, old-fashioned belief in the goodness and rectitude of the American people as my old friend the dean, who, I learned that night, saw the whole thing in terms of black and white. My religious beliefs, my personal problems, my own innate character flaws, and the resultant confusion in my own personal life paralleled almost precisely those of the country at large. I was not part of the youth culture of drugs and free sex, but I opposed the war with all my heart and by extension, it seemed at the time, most of the major institutions in the country, including the university in which I taught. There were voices in me shouting so loud that, like the students later that evening, they drowned out almost everything else.

And so I began to write poetry. Looking back at it now, I think I was probably trying to discover a small place of sanity and order in my life. At least for the time in which I was writing it I could be calm. I could be quiet. I could simply worry with words, trying to get them right. I didn't know how to go about writing poetry, so I simply cut loose, writing as fast as I could, trying to catch the main drift, the central emotion, and see where it took me. I ended up, usually, with four or five single-spaced pages that I would later hack a poem out of the same way Michelangelo was said to hack a statue out of a block of marble. I thought of myself as starting all over again, creating some sort of truth out of random, chaotic experience the same way a reading lamp creates a circle of light in the darkness.

The only things I could write about at first were things that happened when I was a boy. I bought an old place in the country around that same time, and the poems were like that: a form of pastoral, a yearning for a simpler life in the past as seen through the divided, complex perspective of the present. I was looking for something more instinctive, more intuitive, truer to my basic nature than the life I was leading in the city. Poetry, I thought, was what I would use to get in touch with that. I didn't have to know what I was doing in a poem the same way I did in a piece of scholarly research. I could ask questions, profess ignorance, be amazed and full of wonder without having to explain a thing. I kept on with it, and after a while I discovered that I was able to write about other things besides childhood. The circles widened, and I was eventually able to deal with More and Erasmus and other parts of my intellectual life. I also began to publish some poems in pretty good places. Soon I had enough of them for a book that went on to receive a literary award. A friend who specialized in Southern literature began teaching my poetry in place of Alan Tate, whom the students couldn't understand and didn't like anyway. He and I later went on to do a book of conversations about my poetry and poetry in general.

Some time after that, I sold my house in the city, moved to the country, and tried commuting to work a hundred miles each way, thinking to simplify my life and bring the disparate parts together. But first I had a Guggenheim Fellowship that took me to Turkey for a few months and then, the following year, another grant that would allow me to do research in Pakistan. When the American Embassy in Islamabad was burned and all Americans were ordered to leave the country, I returned home a few months early. But by that time the impulse was over. I no longer wanted to write poetry.

And then something happened, and I went back to it again.

*

My wife had decided to go into the cattle business. She didn't know anything about it, of course—and neither did I. But we had some pastures we had kept open by bushogging them a couple of times a year. The fences were broken. The grass was scraggly and needed renewing. But we thought that with a little work we could fix up the place and raise some cattle. So we got in a bulldozer and started clearing.

The man whose bulldozer we happened to hire was a Mormon, one of the very few to be found at that time in the mountains of north Georgia. He was like an outrider, a financial missionary funded by the Mormon Church and sent forth to establish a foothold so others could follow. The Mormon came into town with one wife, and a few weeks later another woman, also claiming to be his wife, moved in and set up housekeeping a few doors away from the first. The Mormon said that he had just divorced the second woman and didn't know what she was doing there. But most people around there didn't believe him. They thought both wives were equally current. The Mormon seemed to have a great deal of money, and that carried a lot of weight—more than the mere suspicion of bigamy. As long as he didn't carry on about it in public, people were willing to ignore it for the sake of what they told themselves might be and probably was his religion.

The Mormon bought the International Harvester Tractor company in town and immediately became one of our leading citizens, a member of the Lions Club, the Optimists' Club, the Kiwanis Club, the Chamber of Commerce, The Oakland Club, and the Apple Valley Association. Besides the tractor dealership, he also bought a brand-new Japanese bulldozer and began clearing land for farmers, mostly for new pastures and apple orchards. He hired an old man named Ray Dalton to operate the bulldozer for him. Ray was born and bred around there, but left when he was still a young man and went out west and traveled up and down the Pacific coast as far south as Mexico and as far north as Alaska, working on construction gangs. He told about chaining two bulldozers together and dropping one off the side of a mountain in order to clear the steepest slopes. Ray had a voice that had been rubbed so raw over the years with dust and whiskey and cigarettes and talking incessantly over the roar of bulldozer engines that you could almost hear the cancer scraping around in there, running up and down his vocal cords on chains as he talked. Ray was a bold, likeable man, full of high spirits and insane gaiety that he kept fine-tuned by drinking steadily on the job. He was long past retirement age and probably wouldn't have been driving a bulldozer for anyone but a Mormon with two known wives already in town and others no doubt on the way. Ray owned a bulldozer of his own, a big, old reconditioned Case, but his two middle-aged boys, Bubba and Bear, were using it to tear down a mountain across the road from their house in order to put in a convenience store on the flat, which they called, when they finally got it built, Dalton's Corner.

Just before coming to clear my place, Ray had been hard at work skimming off the top of a mountain a few miles down the road for what he said were a couple of agronomists from the University of Georgia. He must have cleared fifty acres or more. The owners were going to sow it in grass and put in an apple orchard, he said. A few months later a plane came flying in at night with a load of bright blue canisters containing, the newspapers later reported, five hundred million dollars' worth of cocaine. The plane missed the drop-off site Ray had prepared on top of the mountain and scattered the canisters in the woods and fields all up and down Big Ankle Road.

A woman who lived nearby saw the first one the next morning at breakfast. It looked to be as big as a man, lying off in the distance among the cows in the pasture. She told her husband to go see what it was. She was afraid it might be a bomb. Her husband went out and poked at it and returned home unharmed but completely mystified. His only thought was to call the sheriff.

It turned out that the sheriff's son was the one who was supposed to have picked up the canisters. A number of leading businessmen in town were said to have financed the operation, but none of them was ever indicted because they presumably lied under oath and perjured themselves to the grand jury, which was made up of their friends and neighbors. The only ones who went to jail were the sheriff's son and a couple of young friends of his who had been hired to front for the businessmen.

The sheriff came out and sealed off the area for five or six miles along the road. Then he sent his deputies into the woods and fields to search for blue canisters. He finally had to call out the National Guard, there were so many people roaming around out there, hoping to find one to sell in Atlanta. It was the biggest drug drop in Georgia history.

The agronomists from the University of Georgia apparently did not exist. The impecunious young man who owned the drop site had just bought it a short while before Ray was hired to clear it for him. Before that he had worked as a clerk for the Gold Kist Company, an agribusiness with an outlet in town selling chicken feed, lime, fertilizer, salt blocks, and fence wire to farmers. No one knew where he got the half million dollars to pay for the land or the undisclosed amount he also paid to purchase the concession to operate the local airport.

Shortly after preparing the drop site, Ray appeared at my place one morning and unloaded the big Japanese bulldozer. The Mormon and I agreed on a price, and Ray told me to get up in the cab with him, he wanted the company. It was like sitting on top of a house riding along pushing down anything that got in the way. We rode around knocking down trees and mushing up the place all morning.

At dinnertime Ray came up to the house and sat around on the porch, eating and talking about his adventures. He saw my wife's violin and asked if he could play it for her. He was a good fiddler, he said. And he was. He played it a while, mostly jigs and old fiddle tunes. Then he broke off one of the pegs flush with the neck trying to tune it. He got up without saying a word and handed the violin back to my wife. Then he climbed up on the back of his bulldozer, and rode away into the bushes. I stayed on the porch and watched from a distance as he drove methodically back and forth across the streams in front of the house destroying their contours, grinding them down little by little until they looked like running sores. There used to be rocks in the streambeds. There used to be banks and trees lining them. Now it was mush. I had started off the day with a regular, ordinary-looking place that was a little unkempt and needed clearing and ended up with a disaster area. It looked like a feedlot after ten straight days of rain with the cattle pinned up in there all that time shitting and walking around in it, churning up the mud.

Ray rode around on the bulldozer the next few days drinking and tearing up the place until my wife was ready to throw him out just on general principle.

"The only thing worse than having a bulldozer operator,"

she said, "is having one that drinks on the job and breaks the peg in your violin so you can't even get it out with the pliers, it has to be drilled it's so far up in there."

Ray came up to the house every day he was there and sat on the porch and ate with us and told us lies about bulldozing out west in the Rocky Mountains or up in Alaska, and I was sick at heart. Not with Ray. My wife blamed him, not wanting to blame me, I suppose—or herself, for that matter. But I blamed myself. Even now, many years later, I still have recurrent dreams about people coming in with heavy equipment and tearing up the place, putting in roads and housing developments without my permission.

After Ray left, I did what I could to put the place back together again. I scraped the fields and harrowed them, sowed the high ground in new grass, limed it and fertilized it, and in the fall prayed for hurricanes to hit Florida and ram head-first into the mountains to bring rain so the grass would grow. And it was sometime around then, in the evenings before I went to bed, that I suddenly found myself writing a series of poems about Roman emperors.

I got most of the material from the *Scriptores Historiae Augustae* and Suetonius' *Lives of the Twelve Caesars*, to which I felt free to add whatever I wanted, regarding history not as fact, but as the seedbed of legend and myth. The emperors were monstrous, I thought—monstrous in their pride and vanity, monstrous in their wretched excesses—and the poems were intended to be ironic meditations on the arrogance and pride of men who think of themselves as gods and the way in which great power and wealth corrupt the hearts of those who possess them. "Possessions possess," my wife used to say. She even used to write it in magic marker on the packing boxes the few times we moved, just to remind me.

I was also working at the time on an edition of St. Thomas More's *Dialogue of Comfort Against Tribulation.* This was a book More wrote in prison in order to prepare himself to die. After the *Utopia*, it is probably his greatest work.

Those who were trying to force More to deny his conscience and destroy his soul and sense of integrity were, ironically, old friends of his at court: Cromwell, who had assumed More's position as Lord Chancellor and was in charge of the prosecution; his good friend Audley, the powerful Duke of Norfolk; the sniveling Cranmer, the archbishop of Canterbury; and even King Henry VIII himself, with whom More had walked on the slates at Windsor Castle, observing the stars: "the great king's bluff arm on his neck," in Robert Lowell's phrase, "feeling that friend-slaying, terror-ridden heart / beating under the fat of Aretino." More knew these men for what they were, but he also considered them to be masks, agents or representatives of a more ancient power of evil. "Thus we may see," More said in the book he was writing, "that in such persecutions, it is the midday devil himself that maketh such incursions upon us by the men that are his ministers, to make us fall for fear."

I thought of the emperors as agents or representatives of that same ancient power of evil and used as an epigraph to the poems the same passage More himself used in referring to his enemies: "For we are not contending against flesh and blood, but against the principalities, against the powers, against the world rulers of this present darkness, against the spiritual hosts of wickedness in the heavenly places" (Ephesians 6:12).

I do not literally believe in the devil the same way More did, but I believe in the existence of evil just as I believe in the existence of goodness and virtue. I regard them as fundamental parts of our nature, inextricably bound up together, and they remain the same, I believe, from age to age and culture to culture. I also believe that in certain extreme cases it is possible for a person to be possessed by evil the same way More believed that it was possible for a person to be possessed by a demon.

My thought was to begin each poem with a fragment of Latin that arrested my attention while reading the lives of the emperors, then move on to a literal prose translation, and then finally to the poem itself, which I thought of not as a translation, but as a process of unmasking: a stripping away of the merely human in order to reveal the shadowy outlines of the demonic hidden within. Some of the poems I ended up with seemed hardly more horrifying than the excesses we see all around us today. But that would seem to be the point. Evil wears a human face and is often quite ordinary, even familiar.

The poems were written a while back, when the country was just beginning its decades-long debacle of covetousness and greed. I was attempting at the time to set a new direction for myself and my family, one that would allow us to go our own way and pursue our own values. But it is not quite correct to say that the poems were an attempt to *escape* from the chaos and complexities of the real world. In fact, it was just the opposite. The poems were an attempt to *contain* the real world, or what I found most disturbing about it, in order to come to terms with it. "I thought," Donne says in "The Triple Fool,"

> if I could draw my paines,
> Through Rimes vexation, I should them allay,
> Griefe brought to numbers cannot be so fierce,
> For, he tames it, that fetters it in verse.

I went on to publish some of the poems, and Harcourt Brace Jovanovich (as it was known at the time) agreed to print the entire collection. A few days after the book was accepted, however, I received a letter from Mr. Jovanovich who informed me that despite the editors' recommendations, he had decided not to publish the book because business was bad and he did not want to lose any more money publishing poetry.

I was appalled, of course. But I was also somewhat amused because that was exactly what the poems were about. The coincidence seemed to be overwhelmingly ironic. So I put the book aside. I had thought of writing another volume on saints, who often seem to be as wretched and excessive in their own sublime way as the emperors in theirs. But the moment of writing poetry was over for me. As the place I lived in gradually healed, the need to create a small world of order also waned in me; now, almost ten years later, I have not written another poem.

And yet, looking back at the poems now from this distance, I like to think that one may glimpse in them at times, if only briefly, just for a moment, the obscure outlines of some other face barely visible within the human: monstrous, alien and yet at the same time somehow familiar—a woman in *Vogue* or *Vanity Fair*, who seems to be wearing all her possessions: silk-on-silk-on-cloth-of-gold-on-fur, layer on layer, and all her jewels, rope after rope of pearls, kilos of diamonds, carbuncles larger than her breasts; or some great, important man who betrays his wife and family; some greedy stockbroker or banker or lawyer who ruins those who trust him—people we have known all our lives; our friends or neighbors or, God forbid, even ourselves.

THE EMPERORS

I

ANTONINUS ELAGABALUS

iocabatur sane ita cum servis ut eos iuberet millena pondo
sibi aranearum deferre proposito praemio, collegisseque dici-
tur decem milia pondo aranearum, dicens et hinc intellegen-
dum quam magna esset Roma. . . . claudebat in eiuscemodi
vasis infinitum muscarum, apes mansuetas eas appellans.

He also played jokes with his slaves, as when he offered them a prize for bringing him a thousand pounds of cobwebs. They brought him, it is said, ten thousand pounds, and he remarked that one could tell from that how great Rome is. . . . He would shut up in jars an infinite number of flies and call them tame bees.

Shrouding his godhead in tradesman's attire
Elagabalus trod the maze of the market
Selling figs, aphrodisiacs, and leeches
In sealed boxes labeled *turds*.

There were few buyers.
                                        He therefore
Ordered the slaves of the household
To gather buckets of flies from the shambles
And offered to sell them as tame bees.

And when that venture failed,
He dispatched the army throughout the city
To gather from the darkest corners of Rome
One thousand pounds of cobwebs.

They brought him ten thousand instead
And at one stroke in one afternoon
Cornered the world market in cobwebs,
Causing the Emperor to remark
On the greatness of Rome and its unknown
Acres of filth, its Imperial darkness.

ZENOBIA

ducta est igitur per triumphum ea specie ut nihil pompabilius populo Romano videretur. iam primum ornata gemmis ingentibus, ita ut ornamentorum onere laboraret. fertur enim mulier fortissima saepissime restitisse, cum diceret se gemmarum onera ferre non posse. vincti erant praeterea pedes auro, manus etiam catenis aureis, nec collo aureum vinculum deerat, quod scurra Persicus praeferebat. huic vita ab Aureliano concessa est, ferturque vixisse cum liberis matronae iam more Romanae data sibi possessione in Tiburti.

She was led therefore in such a spectacular triumph that the Roman people had never seen anything so wonderful. She was weighted down, in the first place, with jewels so huge that she labored under the weight of her ornaments. Strong as she was, she often stopped, it is said, and complained that she could not carry her jewelry. Her feet were bound with fetters of gold, her hands with golden manacles. She even had a small gold chain around the neck and a beggar from Persia to carry it in front of her. She was granted her life by Aurelian and is said to have lived with her children like a Roman matron on an estate she was given at Tibur.

Zenobia rose like the star of the East,
Cleopatra redivivus, Queen of Egypt
And Palmyra, relict of Septimius Odaenathus,
Rival of Rome.

               Taken in battle
She was led in triumph and forced
To wear her entire wardrobe. Silk-
On-silk-on-cloth-of-gold-on-fur.
Layer on layer.
               She looked like a thief.

And all her jewels. Rope after rope
Of pearls. Kilos of diamonds. Carbuncles.
Her feet were bound with shackles of gold.
Around her neck, a gold and onyx
Chain, the weight of which was borne by
A passing dervish from Persia, who surmised
That she was being punished for prostitution.
She fell three times before attaining the Capitol,
Where, stripped of her jewels and fine array,
She was made to endure a mock execution,
During which she flung herself from the parapet.

The crowd below snatched at her scalp and pubes
For hair, seeking souvenirs of her greatness.

AELIUS VERUS

dicitur sane tantam habuisse curam flaventium capillorum, ut capiti auri ramenta respergeret, quo magis coma illuminata flavesceret.

He was so proud of his blond hair, it is said, that he used to sprinkle it with gold to make it more yellow and gleam with light.

Verus sprinkled his lovely hair
With gold and crystalline grains of blood.
His hair was blond. It glittered insanely
Like mica.

        One thought of teeth.
And suddenly, unbidden: the image
Of sunlight shattered on water.
Broken.
        Beyond appeal.

CLAUDIUS

in diatem, cui nomen est Hermaneum, recesserat; neque multo post rumore caedis exterritus prorepsit ad solarium proximum interque praetenta foribus vela se abdidit. latentem discurrens forte gregarius miles, animadversis pedibus, studio sciscitandi quisnam esset, adgnovit extractumque et prae metu ad genua sibi accidentem imperatorem salutavit. . . . et quotiens post cibum addormisceret, quod ei fere accidebat, olearum aut palmularum ossibus incessebatur. . . . solebant et manibus stertentis socci induci, ut repente expergefactus faciem sibimet confricaret.

He withdrew into a suite of rooms called the Hermaneum, and a little later, terrified by news of Caligula's murder, crept out on a balcony nearby and hid behind the curtains in front of the door. An ordinary soldier running by saw his feet sticking out and, wanting to know who it was, drew him forth. Recognizing Claudius, the soldier saluted him as emperor while Claudius fell at his feet out of fear. . . . And whenever he went to sleep after dinner, which was quite often, the guests threw olive and date pits at him. . . . They also used to put slippers on his hands when he was snoring and then wake him suddenly so he would rub his face with them.

When Gaius Caligula was finally murdered
And his rage and madness, loosed in the air,
Rushed about among the crowd,
Claudius ran to the Hermaneum
And hid behind some drapes on the wall.

A private soldier started the play
And opened the curtains not on Polonius,
But on a God.
                    Later
When Claudius slept after wine,
Sprawling among the plates on the table,
His friends put slippers on his hands,
And he woke to paws rubbing his face,
The sound of braying in his ears,
For his power was made perfect in weakness.

HADRIANUS

"Hadrianus Augustus Serviano consuli salutem. Aegyptum,
. . . totam didici levem, pendulam et ad omnia famae mo-
menta volitantem. illic qui Serapem colunt Christiani sunt,
et devoti sunt Serapi qui se Christi episcopos dicunt. nemo il-
lic archisynagogus Iudaeorum, nemo Samarites, nemo Chris-
tianorum prebyster non mathematicus, non haruspex, non
aliptes. . . . nihil illis opto, nisi ut suis pullis alantur, quos
quemadmodum fecundant, pudet dicere."

"Hadrian Augustus to the Consul Servianus, greetings. I have discovered . . . Egypt to be completely light-weight, dubious, eager for every shred of gossip. Those who worship Serapis are Christians, and those devoted to Serapis say they are Christian bishops. There is no head man in the Jewish synagogue, no Samaritan, no Christian priest, who is not also an astrologer, soothsayer, or anointer. . . . My only wish for the Egyptians is that they live on their own chickens, which they breed in a way I am ashamed to mention."

"Hadrian Augustus to his brother, Servianus,
Greetings:
                    The Egyptians, I find are light-weight,
Unstable, blown about by the blast
Of men's mouths like the ropes of sand
That restrain the Nile.
                              Those who worship
Serapis are in fact Christian,
And there is hardly a priest,
Jew, Copt, or Christian, who is not
Also an astrologer, soothsayer, or anointer.

The chickens they breed are like great men:
The eggs are buried in dunghills,
And the heat of the sun draws them forth
Like the blessings of god on his beloved Augustus."

JULIUS

dein post solis occasum mulis e proximo pistrino ad vehiculum iunctis occultissimum iter modico comitatu ingressus est. . . . consecutusque cohortis ad Rubiconem flumen, qui provinciae eius finis erat, paulum constitit, ac reputans quantum moliretur, conversus ad proximos: "etiam nunc," inquit, "regredi possumus; quod si ponticulum transierimus, omnia armis agenda erunt." cunctanti ostentum tale factum est. quidam eximia magnitudine et forma in proximo sedens repente apparuit harudine canens; ad quem audiendum cum praeter pastores plurimi etiam ex stationibus milites concurrissent interque eos et aeneatores, rapta ab uno tuba prosilivit ad flumen et ingenti spiritu classicum exorsus pertendit ad alteram ripam. tunc Caesar: "eatur," inquit, "quo deorum ostenta et inimicorum iniquitas vocat. iacta alea est," inquit.

Then after sunset he took some mules from a bakery nearby and, hitching them to a carriage, set out with a small group of friends on a secret journey. . . . Overtaking the army at the Rubicon river, the boundary of his province, he paused for a moment to consider what he was about to do. Turning to those beside him, he said, "Right now we can turn back, but if we cross that little bridge, it will be war." While he was wondering what to do, he was given this sign. A being of great size and beauty suddenly appeared sitting nearby playing on a reed. Shepherds ran to hear, and many soldiers deserted their posts, among them trumpeters. Seizing a trumpet from one of them, the apparition rushed to the river and, raising the war cry with a mighty blast, charged toward the opposite bank. Then Caesar: "Let us go where the signs of the gods and the iniquity of our enemies call. The die is cast."

Taking a span of mules from a tailor
Caesar threaded the eye of the night
And overtook the army at dawn
Beside a stream at the edge of his province

And there he paused, uncertain of fate,
Until he saw on the distant shore
A marvelous being clothed in light
Who played on a reed. The heavens opened
And a voice cried out, "This is my beloved son!"

Caesar took it to refer to himself
And forthwith flung himself in the river
As into his own liquid grave,
Hoping thereby to be rendered immortal.
Thus he began his public life.

II

CARUS, CARINUS, NUMERIÁN

memorabile maxime Cari et Carini et Numeriani hoc habuit imperium, quod ludos populo Romano novis ornatos spectaculis dederunt. . . . nam et neurobaten, qui velut in ventris cothurnatus ferretur, exhibuit, et toichobaten, qui per parietem urso eluso cucurrit, et ursos mimum agentes et item centum salpistas uno crepitu concinentes. . . . exhibuit et ludum Sarmaticum. . . . exhibuit Cyclopea. donatum est Graecis artificibus et gymnicis et histrionibus et musicis aurum et argentum, donata et vestis serica.

The most memorable event in the reign of Carus and Carinus and Numerian were the games and unusual spectacles they presented to the Roman people. . . . They had a rope-walker who walked in his buskins as if on wind and a wall-climber who, eluding the bear, ran up the side of a wall. They also had bears performing a farce and a hundred trumpeters blowing a blast. . . . They had Sarmatian games . . . and a Cyclops performance. The Grecian artists, gymnasts, actors, and musicians, were rewarded with gold and silver and garments of silk.

Numerian is said to have given the City
A troop of bears who performed a farce,
Mouthing the words in shit-stained tunics.

Carus exhibited a rope dancer
Who seemed to tread in his buskins on wind.

Carinus presented a Parthian runner
Who, eluding a leopard, ran up the side
Of a wall while remaining pefectly horizontal.
The leopard ate him on the way down.

One hundred trumpeters were assembled
To blow a blast in a criminal's ear.
His eyes started out of his head.

There were nevertheless Sarmatian games,
A Cyclops performance, and a Grecian magician
Who multiplied loaves of bread,
Gold, silver and silken fish,
To be distributed among the people.

HADRIANUS

amicos ditavit et quidem non petentes, cum petentibus nihil negaret. idem tamen facile de amicis, quidquid insusurrabatur, audivit atque ideo prope cunctos vel amicissimos vel eos, quos summis honoribus evexit, postea ut hostium loco habuit. . . . nam Eudaemoneum prius conscium imperii ad egestatem perduxit, Polaenum et Marcellum ad mortem voluntariam coegit. . . . Ummidium Quadratum et Catilium Severum et Turbonem graviter insecutus est. . . . Antinoum suum, dum per Nilum navigat, perdidit, quem muliebriter flevit. de quo varia fama est, aliis eum devotum pro Hadriano adserentibus, aliis quod et forma eius ostentat et nimia voluptas Hadriani. et Graeci quidem volente Hadriano eum consecraverunt, oracula per eum dari adserentes, quae Hadrianus ipse composuisse iactatur.

He enriched his friends without their asking, and when they asked, he denied them nothing. Still he was ready to listen to rumor and came to consider as enemies almost all those closest to him or those whom he had raised to positions of the highest honor. . . . Eudaemon helped him become emperor, and he reduced him to poverty. Polaenus and Marcellus were driven to suicide. . . . Ummidius Quadratus, Catilius Severus, and Turbo were severely persecuted. . . . He wept like a woman for his lover, Antinous, who was lost while sailing the Nile. There are various stories about what happened. Some say that Antinous swore that he would die for Hadrian; others believe what both Antinous' beauty and Hadrian's excessive lust would suggest. Since Hadrian desired it, some Greeks deified Antinous and claimed that the oracle spoke through him, but Hadrian bragged that he made up the oracles himself.

Hadrian enriched his loved ones with treasure
Beyond the wit of man to dream
What treasure it was.
                    Eudaemon
Was outcast and grew poor in spirit.
Nigiridius, disfigured because of his beauty,
Learned how to mourn.
                    Cicero Afer
Rejoiced in his meekness after torture.
Ummidius Quadratus, Catilius Serverus
Were persecuted for righteousness' sake.

And Antinous, the Emperor's favorite, so loved
His master that he gave up his own life
For him, in fulfillment of the prophesies,
Flinging himself headlong into the Nile
Only to rise from the Tiber a God.

NERO

captus autem modulatis Alexandrinorum laudationibus, qui
de novo commeatu Neapolim confluxerant, plures Alexan-
dria evocavit. neque eo segnius adulescentulos equestris or-
dinis et quinque amplius milia e plebe robustissimae iuven-
tutis undique elegit, qui divisi in factiones plausuum genera
condiscerent—bombos et imbrices et testas vocabant—ope-
ramque navarent cantanti sibi, insignes pinguissima coma et
excellentissimo cultu, puris ac sine anulo laevis.

He was captivated by the rhythmic applause of some Alexandrians who flocked to Naples from a transport that had just arrived, and so he sent for more of them. Just as enthusiastically, he selected some young aristocrats and more than five thousand sturdy young commoners and taught them the new style of applause. Dividing them into teams called the Bees, the Roof Tiles, and the Bricks, he had them cheer for him while he sang. They were noted for their thick hair and fine clothing. Their left hands were bare and without rings.

The Bees, the Roof Tiles, and the Bricks
All had thick hair and fine apparel.
Their left hands were authentically bare.

Each group remained distinct,
And the applause was rhythmic, Alexandrine.

Nero sang like the lark ascending
While the City collapsed to the cries of its people.
Such was the magic of his art.

ANTONINUS ELAGABALUS

exhibiuit parasitis cenas et de vitreis et nonnumquam tot picta mantelia in mensam mittebat, iis edulibus picta quae adponerentur, quot missis esset habiturus, ita ut de acu aut de textili pictura exhiberentur. nonnumquam tamen et tabulae illis pictae exhibebantur, ita ut quasi omnia illis exhiberentur et tamen fame macerarentur.

He served his parasites dinners of glass, sometimes sending to their table embroidered or woven cloths depicting everything he was having to eat, even to the same number of courses. And sometimes they were given paintings of food. It was as if they had been served the whole meal and were still tormented with hunger.

When Elagabalus chose to banquet alone,
The tribe of parasites who joined him at table
Were served with food made of glass
And a series of napkins with every dish
The emperor ate embroidered thereon
According to the number and sequence of courses.

Feeding on shadows, they grew in illusion
Like giants of old, swollen with wind,
Or ancient Jews, who follow their dead Messias,
The Christus, devouring the food of expectation,
While others, too old and wise for that, crept
Among the Imperial hounds, searching for offal.

COMMODUS ANTONINUS

dicitur saepe pretiosissimis cibis humana stercora miscuisse nec abstinuisse gustum alliis, ut putabat, inrisis.

He often mixed human excrement with the most exquisite of foods, it is said, and did not hesitate to taste it himself, thus mocking other men, as he thought.

Commodus Antoninus lifted the lid,
And there was a platter of tetrapharmacum,
A food of which he was singularly fond,
Consisting of pheasant, sow's udder,
Ham, pastry, and the dark aftertaste
Of human excrement.
                              Commodus bent
His head and ate, beckoning his guests
To partake of it with him.
But they held back for fear of dishonor,
And he turned and mocked them, as he thought,
Calling them men of their mother's blood,
Stained like iron before the never-surfeited sea
Belched them forth on their father's shore,
Whence this tainted flesh, this reminder.

III

DIDIUS JULIANUS

fuit praeterea in Iuliano haec amentia, ut per magos pleraque faceret, quibus putaret vel odium populi deleniri vel militum arma compesci. nam et quasdam non convenientes Romanis sacris hostias immolaverunt et carmina profana incantaverunt, et ea quae ad speculum dicunt fieri, in quo pueri praeligatis oculis incantato vertice respicere dicuntur, Iulianus fecit.

And Julianus was so insane as to employ magi to lessen the hate of the people and restrain the power of the army. The magi sacrificed particular victims unknown before to Roman ritual and chanted unholy songs while Julianus did things which, we are told, took place in front of a mirror in which boys were said to gaze with their eyes blindfolded while charms were muttered over their heads.

To lessen the hate of the Roman people
And restrain the army, Didius ordered
Magical rites imported from Asia.

Priests mutilated themselves with slivers of glass.
Pregnant slaves drank quicksilver.
Boys were led to gaze in a mirror,
Eyes bound with bandages,
Charms muttered over their heads,
Until they cried out at the horrors they saw.

When Didius masturbated before it,
The face that appeared was not his own.

SEVERUS

ultima verba eius dicuntur haec fuisse: ". . . senex et pedibus aeger firmum imperium Antoninis meis relinquens. . . ." Fortunam deinde regiam, quae comitari principes et in cubiculis poni solebat, geminare statuerat, ut sacratissimum simulacrum utrique relinqueret filiorium; sed cum videret se perurgueri sub hora mortis, iussisse fertur ut alternis diebus apud filios imperatores in cubiculis Fortuna poneretur. quod Bassianus prius contempsit quam faceret parricidium.

His last words it is said were these: ". . . An old man, lame of foot, I bequeath the empire to my two sons, the Antonini. . . ." He then ordered a replica made of the royal statue of Fortune, which usually accompanies the emperors and is placed in their bedrooms, for he wished each son to have a copy. But when he saw that the hour of death was upon him, he commanded that Fortune be placed in the bedrooms of each of his sons, the Emperors, on alternate days. Bassianus at first held that in contempt. Then he murdered his brother.

His last words it is said were these:
"An old man with crippled feet,
I bequeath the state and the Roman people
To my two sons, the Antonini."

And to show his equal love for each
Ordered the statue of the goddess of Fortune
That stands in the emperor's private chamber
To rotate between them on alternate days
Lest they forget the translation of empire.

So Severus.
               And so it was done
Until Bassianus, the younger son,
Grasped the lesson his father intended,
Opened the casket and murdered his brother.

P. LICINIUS
EGNÁTIUS GÁLLIENUS

haec vita Gallieni fuit. . . . orbem terrarum viginti prope per
tyrannos vastari fecti, ita ut etiam mulieres illo melius im-
perarent. ac ne eius praetereatur miseranda sollertia, veris
tempore cubicula de rosis fecit. de pomis castella composuit.
uvas triennio servavit. hieme summa melones exhibuit. . . .
saepe ad tibicinem processit, ad organum se recepit, cum pro-
cessui et recessui cani iuberet.

Such was the life of Gallienus. . . . that he caused the world to be laid waste by almost twenty pretenders. Even women ruled better than he. But not to pass over his pitiful talents — he used to make couches of roses in the spring of the year. He built castles of apples, preserved grapes for three years, served melons in the depth of winter. . . . He often set out to the sound of pipes and returned to the sound of the organ, ordering music to accompany his coming and going.

The reign of Gallianus was such that the world
Was laid waste by twenty pretenders.
But lest his accomplishments be forgotten, let it
Be shown that he was skilled in constructing tableaux
Composed of the ravished children of slaves.
He also constructed castles of apples,
Ate jeweled fish and pomegranates
Without passing stones in his urine,
And invented a method of weighing his words.
He went forth to the sound of pipes
And returned to the sound of flesh on flesh.
The caged beast in the prison pounding.

GAIUS CALIGULA

templum etiam numini suo proprium et sacerdotes et exco-
gitatissimas hostias instituit. in templo simulacrum stabat
aureum inconicum amiciebaturque cotidie veste, quali ipse
uteretur.

He also established a temple to his own godhead with priests and the finest of sacrifices. In the temple stood a golden statue of the emperor dressed each day in garments identical to those he was wearing.

Because he believed he had no soul,
Only a dream he barely remembered,
He ordered a temple built in his honor
Wherein he exhibited his ideal self,
Perfect in all its properties and proportions,
Crafted in twenty-four carat gold.
He called it his immortal soul.
Dressed each morning by vestal virgins
In clothing such as he himself wore,
It resembled a doll more than a soul.

Caligula marveled at how clean it was.
He stank of urine, semen and blood.
Its armpits were sweet.

Yet he was the dreamer,
                              Caligula said.
It was the dream. He was the foreskin.
It was the glans. Sleek as a whelk,
Polished and bright as a pearl in an oyster.

MARCUS ANTONINUS

tantus autem terror belli Marcomannici fuit ut undique sa-
cerdotes Antoninus acciverit, peregrinos ritus impleverit,
Romam omni genere lustraverit. . . . tanta autem pestilen-
tia fuit ut vehiculis cadavera sint exportata sarracisque. . . .
multa quidem milia pestilentia comsumpsit. . . . cuidam, qui
diripiendae urbis occasionem cum quibusdam consciis re-
quirens de caprifici arbore in Campo Martio contionabundus
ignem de caelo lapsurum finemque mundi affore diceret, si
ipse lapsus ex arbore in ciconiam verteretur, cum statuto
tempore decidisset atque ex sinu ciconiam emisisset, per-
ducto ad se confesso veniam daret.

There was such fear of war with the Marcommani that priests were summoned from all directions to perform foreign rites and purify the city in every way possible. . . . But the pestilence was so bad that the dead were hauled off in carts and wagons. . . . Many thousands were consumed by the plague. . . . And one man, searching with friends for a way to loot the city, spoke non-stop from the wild fig tree on the Campus Martius to the effect that fire would fall from the sky and the world would end if he were to tumble out of the tree and turn into a stork. And finally, at the time appointed, he did in fact fall from the tree and release a stork that he had hidden under his coat. Taken before the emperor, the man confessed and was forgiven.

So great was Rome's fear of the Marcomanni
That Marcus ordered lustral processions
To proceed in all directions at once
Throughout the City. But instead of victory
In battle, the gods bestowed
A pestilence that destroyed one-third
Of the population and called forth a prophet
Who immediately climbed to the top of a tree
On the Campus Martius and, making a nest,
Issued bird-like prayers and imprecations,
Mostly about the end of the world
And what would happen if he were arrested.

When Marcus ordered him arrested,
The man turned into a stork, as predicted,
And lumbered flapping back to heaven.

The same day the pestilence ceased
And the war ended. Thus Rome was saved
By the wisdom, foresight, and perspicuity
Of Marcus, Pontifex Maximus.

IV

PERTINAX

signa interitus haec fuerunt: ipse ante triduum quam occide-
retur in piscina sibi visus est videre hominem cum gladio in-
festantem. et ea die qua occisus est negabant in oculis eius
pupulas cum imaginibus, quas reddunt, spectantibus visas.

These were the signs of his death. Three days before he was killed, he thought he saw in a fish pond a man attacking him with a sword. On the day he died, there were said to be no pupils in his eyes. Those who looked into them saw nothing there, not even reflections.

Pertinax was warned of his death in this fashion.
Three days before he killed himself
He looked into a pool of water
And imagined he saw what looked like a man
Strike at his face with an upturned rake.

On the day of his death, his lovers reported,
His eyes were so blue they thought he was blind.
Nothing was there, not even reflections,
Only the pupilless gaze of the iris
And inside, as inside a pool of still water,
A being that struck at them with a rake.

ANTONINUS PIUS

atque ita conversus quasi dormiret, spiritum reddidit apud Lorium. . . . fuit statura elevata decorus. sed cum esset longus et senex incurvareturque, tiliaciis tabulis in pectore positis fasciabatur, ut rectus incederet. senex etiam, antequam salutores venirent, panem siccum comedit ad sustentandas vires.

And so he turned as if going to sleep and rendered up his spirit at Lorium. . . . He was a tall, handsome man, so tall that when he was stooped with age, he had himself tied up in a bundle of linden laths to enable him to walk upright. He also ate dry bread in his old age to build up his strength before receiving visitors.

Antoninus Pius died in his seventieth
Year at Lorium after eating
(In imitation of Cato) a meal
Consisting of dry bread and beans.
He groaned and turned his face to the wall.

The women who came and prepared the body
Discovered hidden under his toga
Thin strips of oak tied to his torso
Running up from his waist to his armpits
Like staves or splints on a broken bone.

Those who saw it averted their eyes
As from the sprawl of his genitals.
Both seemed absurd.
                              The body's secret shame,
The mind's dark schemes and purposes.

ANTONINUS ELAGABALUS

et praedictum eidem erat a sacerdotibus Syris biothanatam
se futurum. paraverat igitur funes blatta et serico et cocco
intortos, quibus, si necesse esset, laqueo vitam finiret. para-
verat et gladios aureos, quibus se occideret, si aliqua vis ur-
gueret. paraverat et in cerauniis et hyacinthis et in smarag-
dis venena, quibus se interimeret, si quid gravius inmineret.
fecerat et altissimam turrem substratis aureis gemmatisque
ante se tabulis, ex qua se praecipitaret, dicens etiam mortem
suam pretiosam esse debere et ad speciem luxuriae, ut dice-
retur nemo sic perisse. sed nihil ista valuerunt. nam, ut dixi-
mus, et occisus est per scurras et per plateas tractus et sordis-
sime per cloacas ductus et in Tiberim submissus est.

Syrian priests foretold that he would die a violent death. So he had cords prepared, woven of purple and scarlet silk, to garrote himself with if necessary. And he prepared golden swords to kill himself with if he were attacked, and poisons in ceraunites and sapphires and emeralds designed to take his life if he were hard pressed. And he built an enormous tower to fling himself off, constructed of boards gilded and set with jewels under his own direction. For even his death, he said, ought to be expensive and luxurious. He did not want it said that anyone had ever died so well. But none of that mattered, for, as we have said, he was killed by soldiers of the guard, dragged through the streets, drawn most foully through sewers, and thrown in the Tiber.

When the Emperor Elagabalus
Was told by a Syrian oracle
That he would die a violent death,
He had a special noose prepared
Of woven blue and scarlet silk
And a Nubian slave to carry it beside him
By day and sleep with it by his side
At night so that he could be garroted
In Imperial purple by his own shadow.

He also had golden swords prepared,
Poisons from Egypt, conclusions infinite
Of a thousand easy ways to die
Coiled in the cunning hollow of a ring.
Carnelians, sapphires, emeralds, diamonds,
Carbuncles rounder than a woman's breast
Contrived to suck the blood asleep.
And in the courtyard built a tower
Higher than the topmost turrets of Rome,
The swirling grain of the scaffolding
Gilded in patterns of solid gold,
Steps inlaid with precious stone,
Jade and lapis lazuli.
And there he would run when death
Followed after and fling himself off
So that all men forever would be struck dumb

By the wonder and the beauty and the glory of his going,
The elegance and mastery of Elagabalus,
The last of the line of the Antonines.

But when the time came for his death
And Fate led the Praetorian Guard
To attack the palace and free the state,
They found the emperor coiled like a snake
Inside the cunning hollow of a privy.
When he was killed, he fell in the pit.
The soldiers dug him out
And lashed him to the back of an axle
And dragged him through the squares of the city,
Through the dust and debris of the track at the Circus.
Then they stuffed him in a sewer,
But he got stuck halfway in,
And they weighted him with stones instead
And threw him off the Aemilian Bridge
So no one could ever bury the body.

Those who killed him spoke no Latin.
The Senate ordered his name erased
From public works and public record.
 But the people remembered.

They called him
Big Ass and Emperor Shit Face
And told the story from father to son
While the story held up.
Then they forgot him.

Except for some.
They are the ones
Who are haunted in sleep by a freckled hand
That holds a severed head like a lantern
And a voice that says, over and over,
The time is free.

HADRIANUS

mathesin sic scire sibi visus est ut vero kalendis Ianuariis scripserit, quid ei toto anno posset evenire, ita ut eo anno quo periit usque ad illam horam qua est mortuus scripserit quid acturus esset. . . . Hadrianus autem ultimo vitae taedio iam adfectus gladio se transfigi a servo iussit. . . . et moriens quidem hos versus fecisse dicitur.

> *Animula vagula blandula*
> *hospes comesque corporis,*
> *quae nunc abibis in loca*
> *pallidula rigida nudula?*
> *nec ut soles dabis iocos.*

He considered himself so skilled in astrology that on the first of January he wrote down everything that could happen to him the following year, and so, the year he died, he wrote down everything he was going to do down to the very hour of his death. . . . Hadrian was now totally disgusted with life and ordered a servant to run him through with a sword. . . . He is said to have written these lines when he was dying.

> *Sweet little soul, wanderer,*
> *friend and inmate of my body,*
> *where are you going now,*
> *pale, stiff, half-naked?*
> *Besides, you don't joke around*
> *like you used to.*

Hadrian was so perfected in knowledge
He knew the secret wishes of the stars
Before they imprinted the air with desire.
He saw the planets wheeling in orbit
Like forms of thought already possessed.

And so it was on the day appointed
He foretold all that was going to happen.
Dismissing his slaves, he sharpened the stylus,
And this is what he wrote.

Disgust like a tether crusts my body.
Gold or garbage, I cannot die.
The quick of my soul, that small beast,
Jibbers like the flame of a candle.
Then the dark.
                    Myself alone.